THE COMPLETE KETO DIET
BOOK FOR WOMEN

The Complete Beginners Keto Diet Cookbook
with Easy to Make and Delicious Recipes

OLIVIA C. SMITH

Table of Contents

Keto Dinner Recipes 77

CONCLUSION 96

INTRODUCTION

The keto diet is so different from other weight loss diet plans that it tends to spark concern, particularly regarding women's health.

There is no doubt that carb restriction can promote substantial amounts of fat loss for many women, but its impact on hormone levels, fertility, pregnancy, and menopause is often misunderstood.

This naturally begs the question: Do keto weight loss results come at a cost, or is the diet a win-win for women's health? To help answer this critical question, we've developed this comprehensive guide to keto for women.

What is the Keto Diet?

A keto diet is a restrictive eating style that changes the type of fuel your body uses. The diet starves the body of glucose, the primary source of energy that comes from carbohydrates. Legumes, bread, pasta, cereal, starchy vegetables like potatoes, dairy foods and sweets aren't typically on the menu.

Without glucose, the liver transforms stored fat into chemicals called ketone bodies, which are then consumed by the brain and body as energy.

To fuel ketosis, the body needs more fat, which is why a **classic keto diet** includes:

- 90% of calories are from fat (incredibly saturated fat such as red meat, whipping cream, and butter).
- 6% of calories from protein (too much protein throws a monkey wrench into ketosis).
- 4% of calories from carbohydrates.

Modified keto diets typically include less fat, more protein and often more carbohydrates than a classic keto diet. The ratios vary widely, depending on the diet:

- 70% to 87% of calories from fat.
- 10% to 15% of calories from protein.
- 3% to 15% of calories from carbs.

"Both the classic keto and modified keto diets are far from how most people normally eat. Most of our calories – around 45% to 65% – normally come from carbs. These diets drive the carbs down to around 10% and limit so many food groups that it becomes almost impossible to follow this long-term eating pattern," says Liz Weinandy, the lead outpatient registered dietitian at Ohio State University Wexner Medical Center.

What is Ketosis?

Ketosis is a metabolic state with a high concentration of ketones in the blood. This happens when fat provides most of the fuel for the body, and there's limited access to glucose. Glucose (blood sugar) is the preferred fuel source for many cells in the body.
Ketosis is most often associated with ketogenic and deficient carb diets. It also happens during pregnancy, infancy, fasting and starvation.

For ketosis to start, you generally need to eat fewer than 50 grams of carbs and sometimes as little as 20 grams per day. However, the exact carb intake that will cause ketosis varies between individuals.

To do this, you may need to remove certain food items from your diet, such as:

- grains
- candy
- sugary soft drinks

You also have to cut back on:

- legumes
- potatoes
- fruit

When eating a very low-carb diet, hormone insulin levels decrease, and fatty acids are released from body fat stores in large amounts.

Many of these fatty acids are transported to the liver, oxidized and turned into ketones (or ketone bodies). These molecules can provide energy for the body.

Unlike fatty acids, ketones can cross the blood-brain barrier and provide energy for the brain without glucose.

Is Keto Safe, Healthy, and Effective for All Women?

According to the research literature and the abundance of success stories, the keto diet can be a safe and effective weight loss approach that helps improve many ordinary women's health struggles.

The keto diet may be most effective for women who are struggling with:

- Weight loss and yo-yo dieting
- Epilepsy
- Polycystic ovarian syndrome (PCOS)
- Yeast overgrowth
- Insulin resistance, type 1 diabetes, or type 2 diabetes
- Heart disease
- Neurodegenerative diseases such as Alzheimer's or Parkinson's
- Certain forms of cancer

That being said, some women may find a different low-carb approach better for their overall health. This may include women who are:

- Female athletes/lifters that notice a significant drop in performance and recovery on keto 2-3 months.
- Struggling with a hypothyroid condition that isn't responding well to keto.
- Notice a worsening in blood lipid levels when they eat high saturated fat.
- Gain fat on a keto diet after tracking macros
- Have stopped menstruating or are having an irregular cycle
- Are pregnant or breastfeeding before their body has adapted to keto
- Notice an increase in menopause-related symptoms after 2-3 months of keto

Regardless of your current health condition, we must also keep in mind that the success of any diet depends significantly on the person. It will take some self-experimentation before you find out what approach to keto is the right fit for you.

Although this implies there will be some ups and downs along the way, this also means that you are not destined to be less healthy and gain fat as you age. Even if you are over 50 and struggling with menopause, you will still be able to achieve your health and weight loss goals.

Keto and weight loss for women

One of the main reasons why women turn to the keto diet is to lose excess body fat. Some research suggests the keto diet may be an effective way to encourage fat loss in the female population. Studies have shown that following a keto diet may aid weight loss by increasing fat-burning and decreasing calorie intake and hunger-promoting hormones like insulin, may help encourage fat loss. For example, one study in 45 women with ovarian or endometrial cancer found that women who followed a ketogenic diet for 12 weeks had significantly less total body fat and lost 16% more belly fat than women assigned to a low-fat, high-fiber diet.

Another study in adults with obesity that included 12 women demonstrated that following a very low-calorie ketogenic diet for 14 weeks significantly reduced body fat, decreased food cravings, and improved female sexual function.

Additionally, a review of 13 randomised controlled trials — the gold standard in research — that included a population of 61% women found that participants who followed ketogenic diets lost 2 pounds (0.9 kg) more than those on low-fat diets after 1 to 2 years.

Although research supports the use of this shallow carb way of eating to enhance fat loss in the short term, keep in mind that there's currently a lack of studies exploring the long-term effects of the keto diet on weight loss.

Plus, some evidence suggests that the weight-loss-promoting benefits of the keto diet drop off around the 5-month mark, which may be due to its restrictive nature.

Moreover, some research shows that less restrictive low carb diets may result in comparable effects and are easier to sustain long term.

For example, a study that included 52 women found that low and moderate carb diets that contained 15% and 25% carbs reduced body fat and waist circumference over 12 weeks, similar to a ketogenic diet that contained 5% carbs.

Plus, the higher-carb diets were more straightforward for the women.

Does Keto Work for Middle-Aged Women?

There is a lot of research to substantiate the efficacy of keto for women over 50, but most of it is not geared toward its usefulness for losing weight. Researchers and even doctors recommend keto diets to treat various ailments and conditions, but little scientific research has studied its effects on weight loss.

However, there is an abundance of circumstantial evidence to support that a keto diet can help you lose weight, even when you're over 50.

When you restrict carbohydrate intake and maintain a state of ketogenesis, your body naturally turns to fat as its primary energy source. If you also maintain a caloric deficit while on a keto diet, your fat stores will be the primary target for fuel instead of carbohydrates, ultimately leading to weight loss.

As such, many people who struggle to burn that stubborn belly fat find that a keto diet works wonders to prepare their bodies to pull energy from their stored fat.

A study published in the Journal of Women's Health found that keto for women over 50 is safe and effective and can aid in weight loss. The study involved over 65 women, averaging 54 years old. After 12 weeks of following a strict ketogenic diet and eating at a caloric deficit, 60% of the participants lost at least 10% of their body weight.

Does Keto Cause Menopause?

Keto and menopause – two words women might not connect as they reach the transition that ends most estrogen production, menstrual cycles and the reproductive years. But keto and menopause are getting lots of attention now that the ketogenic or keto diet has become a popular eating style. "The keto diet has been around for a long time, and there are certain benefits for menopausal women. But there are many downsides, too," says Dr. Michael Tahery, an obstetrician and urogynecologist based in Los Angeles.

Keto and Menopause: Benefits

Some people turn to keto for menopause to address physical changes and menopause symptoms. For example, without estrogen, metabolism slows, and the body redistributes fat. "Weight collects in the abdomen, even if there hasn't been weight gain," Tahery notes.

Falling estrogen levels also cause menopause symptoms that can last up to seven years, including:

- Hot flashes and night sweats.
- Mood changes.
- Fatigue.
- Difficulty sleeping.
- Fuzzy thinking.
- Vaginal dryness.

Theoretically, the fat-rich ketogenic diet may reduce some menopause symptoms. "Fat is a precursor for estrone, a weak type of estrogen produced by fat cells," Taher says. "The more fat you consume, the more estrogen you'll have in your system. It may contribute to fewer hot flashes, mood changes and fatigue."

Keto may help you:

- Lose weight, reducing your risk of developing heart disease, joint problems and cancer.

- Reduce blood glucose levels, reducing the risk for Type 2 diabetes.
- Improve insulin sensitivity, making this hormone that shepherds glucose to cells more effective.

However, it's important to note that the benefits of keto and menopause are believed to be short-term only. For example, weight loss may result from losing fluids as sugar stores in the body are emptied. "The keto diet acts as a diuretic," Weinandy says.

You may regain the weight as soon as you go off the diet if you don't exercise or reduce the calories you consume.

What to Eat on a Keto Diet?

Keto stresses higher consumption of fat and reduced intake of starch. This can make meal preparation difficult, as many high carbohydrate foods are not considered keto-friendly—such as wheat, bread, starchy vegetables, and berries.

In comparison, carbohydrates tend to be the majority of most people's diets, meaning you have to find a keto substitute or adjust the way you think about food in general. Some of the better staples for any keto diet should have safe carbohydrate replacements. A lot of veggies work well for this, like:

- Cauliflower rice
- Mashed cauliflower
- Portobello mushroom "buns."
- Spaghetti squash
- Zucchini (courgette) noodles (or "zoodles")
- Lettuce wraps

To keep your nutrition in order, most of your keto diet should consist of nutrient-rich carbohydrate vegetables, high-quality proteins, and healthy fats to ensure you have the right balance and overall enough nutrition to keep you moving.

Keto Food List

Here is a brief overview of what you should and shouldn't eat on the keto diet:

Do Not Eat

- Grains – Wheat, corn, rice, cereal, etc.
- Sugar – honey, agave, maple syrup, etc.
- Fruit – apples, bananas, oranges, etc.
- Tubers – potato, yams, etc.

Do Eat

- Meats – fish, beef, lamb, poultry, eggs, etc.
- Low-carb vegetables – spinach, kale, broccoli, and other low-carb veggies.
- High-fat dairy – hard cheeses, high-fat cream, butter, etc.
- Nuts and seeds – macadamias, walnuts, sunflower seeds, etc.
- Avocado and berries – raspberries, blackberries, and other low glycemic impact berries
- Sweeteners – stevia, erythritol, monk fruit, and other low-carb sweeteners.
- Other fats – coconut oil, high-fat salad dressing, saturated fats, etc.

Healthy Fats

When following a high-fat, relatively low-carb ketogenic (keto) diet, it is essential to note that not all fats are equivalent.

Few types of fat are healthier for you than others, and you must load your plate with the most nutritious choices to meet your fitness goals.

Here are 14 safe types of fat to indulge in the keto diet.

1. Avocados and avocado oil
2. Nuts
3. Nut and seed butter
4. Flax seeds
5. Hemp hearts
6. Chia seeds
7. Olives and cold-pressed olive oil
8. coconuts and unrefined coconut oil
9. Cacao nibs
10. Full-fat Greek yogurt
11. Whole eggs
12. Fatty fish
13. Butter
14. Cheese

What can I eat?

Cheese: Brie, cheddar, manchego, cream cheese, you name it. A diet that not only requires cheese but supports it, too.

Beef brisket: Taste this southern favourite with the homemade coleslaw side.

Spinach: skip starchy root veggies such as carrots or potatoes; instead, use keto-friendly greens such as spinach, broccoli, or kale. Use spinach to make a sandwich, or add a pinch to your morning smoothie.

Bacon: Serve with fried eggs on the foot (made from pastured, organic whole eggs).

Yoghurt: You can find your sugar cravings don't go away right away, so enjoy a bowl of yoghurt or cottage cheese topped with berries to alleviate your cravings early on.

Cheeseburger: a keto diet that prefers fatter foods over lean meats, so don't be afraid to bite into a juicy burger –miss the bun. Prepare for grass-fed ground beef and enjoy a bed of lettuce.

Whole-fat milk: put a splash in your morning coffee, but be vigilant before taking a glass of whole-fat milk for breakfast – although high in fat, it is often high in carbs and should be eaten in moderation.

Chicken thighs: fried chicken thighs are a simple meal for dinner. While this meal will take at least 30 minutes to cook in the oven, it will take less than five minutes.

Stevia: Steer clear of sugar and artificial sweeteners and satisfy your sweet tooth with stevia instead.

What food can you eat on the Keto Diet?

Fatty animal protein: meat, bacon, eggs, poultry with skin and fish

Oils and natural fats: Olive, canola and palm oil, and cacao butter latte

Vegetables: Spinach, kale, lettuce, broccoli, and cucumbers

What food can't you eat on Keto Diet?

Alcohol: Not recommended during the ketosis phase

Sugar: This includes artificial sweeteners (use stevia instead).

What foods should you limit on the Keto Diet?

Carbohydrates: Bread and pasta

Starchy root veggies: Potatoes, carrots, and turnips

Benefits of the keto diet?

The ketogenic diet originated as a tool for treating neurological diseases such as epilepsy. Studies have now shown that the diet can have benefits for a wide variety of different health conditions:

Heart disease: The ketogenic diet can help improve risk factors like body fat, HDL (good) cholesterol levels, blood pressure, and blood sugar.

Cancer: The diet is currently being explored as an additional treatment for cancer because it may help slow tumour growth.

Alzheimer's disease: The keto diet may help reduce symptoms of Alzheimer's disease and slow its progression.

Epilepsy: Research has shown that the ketogenic diet can cause significant reductions in seizures in epileptic children.

Parkinson's disease: Although more research is needed, one study found that the diet helped improve symptoms of Parkinson's disease.

Polycystic ovary syndrome: The ketogenic diet can help reduce insulin levels, which may play a key role in polycystic ovary syndrome.

Brain injuries: Some research suggests that the diet could improve outcomes of traumatic brain injuries.

How does it help the immune system?

A recent study was conducted where the researchers fed the Keto diet (low-carb, high-fat diet) to a group of mice infected with flu virus. The report revealed that the group of mice who were given a Keto diet showed a higher rate of survival in comparison to the group that was on a regular high-carb diet. The researchers found that the Keto one led to immune-system cells releasing mucus around lung cell linings. The mucus produced helped trap the flu virus quickly before it could worsen.

According to the researchers, inflammasomes (activators of the immune system) can lead to harmful responses in the host's immune system. The great news is that the ketogenic diet is able to prevent the formation of these unwanted inflammasomes, which eventually helps to strengthen immunity.

Is the Keto Diet a heart-healthy diet?

Low-carb diets like keto may have some heart health benefits. A systematic review of randomised controlled trials comparing low-carb and low-fat diets in overweight and obese patients examined outcomes for nearly 1,800 patients in 17 studies with short-term (less than one year) follow-up. Low-carb diets were associated with significantly more significant weight reduction and significantly lower predicted risk of heart disease tied to hardening of the arteries than low-fat diets, according to the study published in October 2015 in the journal PLOS One.

Dr. Eric Westman, director of the Duke Lifestyle Medicine Clinic and an expert in low-carb and keto diets, recommends the keto diet for some of his patients with heart disease. That, he says, is because the metabolic syndrome – a cluster of symptoms including high triglycerides and low "good" HDL cholesterol, high blood pressure, and high blood sugar, linked to heart disease and diabetes – is caused by a diet that's high in processed carbs and low in healthy fats. He sees improved triglyceride and HDL levels in patients on the keto diet.

Other heart risk factors like high blood pressure may improve on the keto diet. However, anyone with an existing heart condition who goes on a diet should be monitored by their healthcare providers.

Can the Keto Diet prevent or control diabetes?

Research suggests that people with type 2 diabetes can slim down and lower their blood sugar levels with the keto diet. In one study, people with type 2 lost weight, needed less medication and lowered their A1c when they followed the keto diet for a year.
If you're insulin resistant - which means you have higher blood sugar levels because your body isn't responding correctly to the hormone insulin -- you could benefit from nutritional ketosis because your body will need and make less insulin.

Fewer studies are looking at the keto diet for people with type 1 diabetes. One small study found that it helped people with type 1 lower their A1c levels, but we need more research to get a complete picture of the diet's effects.
Remember that most studies have only looked at the short-term results of the keto diet. It's unclear if it works as a long-term way to manage your diabetes.
If you decide to try the keto diet, be aware that it may be hard to stick to. The plan's meager amount of carbs is a significant change for many people. It also can make you feel tired for a few weeks until your body adapts. To make it a success, it's a good idea to make a meal plan you can follow, including keto-friendly meals and snacks to keep on hand.

Does the Keto Diet allow for restrictions and preferences?

Most people can customise the Keto diet according to their needs. Check individual preferences for more information.

Supplement recommended?

A daily vitamin with minerals, including potassium and magnesium, can fill in potential gaps while following keto.
Vegetarian or Vegan: It's possible to adapt the keto diet for vegetarians or vegans, but it's more challenging. Keto-vegan and vegetarian recipes are available on the Healthful Pursuit site.
Gluten-Free: Yes. The keto diet already avoids high-gluten, high-carb foods such as wheat bread, cookies, and pasta. Many nut butter, a keto staple, are also gluten-free.
Low-Salt: Keto can lend itself to a low-salt approach if you avoid processed meats such as sausage and bacon.
Kosher: Yes. Kosher-keto recipes are available in cookbooks and on Facebook.
Halal: It's up to you to prepare meals within guidelines.

What types of meals should you eat on the Keto Diet?

If you crave fat, you're in luck. Start your day with a double "rocket fuel" latte, if you like – and don't skimp on the cacao butter. Lunch on ground turkey patties with a slaw or some sausage links. Keto is one diet where you're encouraged to bypass leaner ground beef and dig into fatty chicken thighs instead of skinless breasts.

Prefer to go meatless? That's entirely possible, mainly if you concentrate on low-carb veggies. Slather on some mayo for a tasty fat boost. As you become more comfortable, you may experiment with exotic vegetable choices like kohlrabi. Fattier fish like salmon will help meet keto requirements for moderate protein and high fat if you include fish-based meals.

Will the Keto Diet help you lose weight?

Recent studies focusing on keto diets suggest some advantages for short-term weight loss. It's still too soon to tell whether people maintain long-term weight loss from ketogenic diets.

In its 2016 report "Healthy Eating Guidelines & Weight Loss Advice," the Public Health Collaboration, a U.K. nonprofit, evaluated evidence on low-carbohydrate, high-fat diets. (The keto diet falls under the LCHF umbrella.) Among 53 randomised clinical trials comparing LCHF diets to calorie-counting, low-fat diets, most studies showed more significant weight loss for the keto-type diets and more beneficial health outcomes. The collaboration recommends weight-loss guidelines that include a low-carbohydrate, high-fat diet of natural (rather than processed) foods as an acceptable, effective, and safe approach.

A small Feb. 20, 2017, study looked at the impact of a six-week ketogenic diet on physical fitness and body composition in 42 healthy adults. The study, published in Nutrition & Metabolism, found a mildly negative impact on physical performance in endurance capacity, peak power, and faster exhaustion. Overall, researchers concluded, "Our findings lead us to assume that a [ketogenic diet] does not impact physical fitness in a clinically relevant manner that would impair activities of daily living and aerobic training." The "significant" weight loss of about 4.4 pounds, on average, did not affect muscle mass or function.

How easy is the Keto Diet to follow?

If you love morning toast, whole-wheat pasta, pizza, and sugary desserts, you could struggle on the keto diet. You'll need time to prepare and educate yourself; the first week won't be much fun.

How much should you exercise on the Keto Diet?

You should stay physically active to benefit from the keto diet most. You might need to take it more accessible during the early ketosis period, especially if you feel tired or lightheaded. Walking, running, aerobics, weightlifting, training with kettlebells, or whatever workout you prefer will further boost your energy. You can find books and online resources on how to adapt Keto meals or snacks for athletic training.

Is the Keto Diet nutritious?

Experts had enough reservations to place the keto diet way down in this category with its combination of unusually high fat and shallow carb content. Experts expressed particular concern for people with liver or kidney conditions, who should avoid it altogether. The jury is still out on whether Keto offers more potential health risks or benefits for people with heart conditions or diabetes. With the variety of Keto versions, food choices, and different cycling methods in and out of the diet, hormonal and other changes can vary widely.

Recipe Notes

We wanted to make it as simple as possible for you to get in the kitchen and rustle up something special so you will find each recipe in an easy-to-follow format.
Remember, this diet is designed to rekindle your love of food, not extinguish it with rules and regulations, so don't be afraid to experiment.
Use the ingredients as general guidelines and follow the instructions as best you can. You may not get everything the perfect first time, every time, but that is what makes it yours!
Keep at it for 30 days of eating, and you will no doubt establish a few firm favourites you can turn into your speciality dishes over time.
Each recipe ends with a breakdown of critical nutritional information, including the number of calories and amount of fats, carbohydrates and protein.
Again, this isn't to be obsessed over. Food is something to be enjoyed, so if you are going to note your intake levels, make it a general estimate.

This cookbook is full of fun and flavour and doesn't take stuff too seriously. The food is entering your mouth, not a modelling contest, and we don't like to encourage an unhealthy obsession with the presentation. So cook expert: tent, and enjoy.
Once you start loving what you are eating, mealtimes will become something to look forward to. Take this as encouragement: go forth and cook to your heart's content!

Things to remember

A healthy diet is not a solution to anything In and of itself; it must be applied as part of a healthy lifestyle to see maximum results.
Think of the ketogenic diet as the foundation of your new body. If you want to build something extraordinary on top of it, design your lifestyle with that goal.
Cutting out junk food goes without saying, as does ditching bad habits such as smoking and drinking. Exercise, too, takes you to heights you never thought possible.
So, as you explore these delectable dishes and embark on the keto diet, try not to neglect other areas of responsibility.
Let this be the start of something great!

28-Days Keto Diet Weight Loss Challenge

Now, the moment you've been waiting for — the meal plan! In this chapter, you'll find a 28-day meal plan for the standard ketogenic diet, divided into four weeks. Every day, you'll follow the plan to eat breakfast, lunch, and dinner, as well as a snack or dessert with a calorie range between 1,800 and 2,000.

One thing I want to mention before you get started is net carbs.

Many people who follow the ketogenic diet prefer to track net carbs rather than total carbs. To calculate net carbs, you simply take the total carb count of the meal and subtract the grams of fibre since fibre cannot be digested. As I mentioned in my first book, I prefer to track total carbs, but I have included the grams of fibre and net carbs in these recipes so you can choose which way to go.

Personally, l prefer more buffer when it comes to the carb count because I want to reduce the number of obstacles keeping me from ketosis. Many of my readers and friends have raised this point, and you can be sure quite a few nights or afternoons were spent in heated debate! Okay, it wasn't that serious, but suffice it to say that a lot of discussion went into this topic. Therefore, I thought giving you a say in this net carb-total carb debate might be better. You get to choose whichever you prefer. In my personal opinion, when you are in the initial stages of trying to enter ketosis, keeping your total carb count in mind is probably one of the better practices you can adopt. A 20 to 50gram range of carbs would usually work to push the body into a ketogenic state.

After you have gotten keto-adapted and the body gets used to burning fat for fuel, you start bringing net carbs into the equation.

Remember the calorie range for these meal plans — if you read my first book and calculated your daily caloric needs, you may need to adjust. If you're trying the ketogenic diet for the first time, however, it may be easiest to follow the plan as is until you get the hang of it.

The first week of this 28-day meal plan is designed to be incredibly simple in terms of meal prep so we can focus on learning which foods to eat and which to avoid on the ketogenic diet — that's why you'll find more smoothies and soups here than in the following weeks. If you finish the first week and feel like you still need some time to adjust to keto, feel free to repeat it before moving on to week two. The meal plans also consider leftovers and the yields of various recipes so that you have minimal wages from your efforts in the kitchen. So, without further ado, let's look at the meal plans.

28-Days Keto Diet Weight Loss Challenge

First Week Meal Plan

Day	Breakfast	Lunch	Dinner
Sunday	Keto egg muffins (Page No. 24)	Special Bacon Sandwich (Page No. 65)	Grilled Chicken Thighs Rosemary (Page No. 77)
Monday	Keto Coffee (Page No. 48)	Blueberry Smoothie (Page No. 58)	Crispy Almond Chicken with Tomato (Page No. 89)
Tuesday	Bulletproof Coffee (Page No. 27)	Garlic Butter Chicken (Page No. 55)	Strawberries smoothie (Page No. 85)
Wednesday	Egg & Sausage Breakfast (Page No. 23)	Coconut Chicken Curry (Page No. 50)	Broccoli Cheddar Soup (Page No. 81)
Thursday	Chocolate Coconut Crunch Smoothie (Page No. 44)	Creamy Zucchini Noodles (Page No. 68)	Creamiest Chocolate Dessert (Page No. 91)
Friday	Blueberry Breakfast Smoothie (Page No. 33)	Mushrooms & Cream Cheese (Page No. 61)	Crispy Chicken with Cheese Sauce (Page No. 82)
Saturday	Egg on Avocado (Page No. 45)	Tantalising Tuna & Spinach Mix (Page No. 54)	Chicken Avocado Creamy Salad (Page No. 84)

28-Days Keto Diet Weight Loss Challenge

Second-Week Meal Plan

Day	Breakfast	Lunch	Dinner
Sunday	Blueberry Breakfast Smoothie (Page No. 33)	Mushrooms & Cream Cheese (Page No. 61)	Crispy Chicken with Cheese Sauce (Page No. 82)
Monday	Keto Coffee (Page No. 48)	Blueberry Smoothie (Page No. 58)	Crispy Almond Chicken with Tomato (Page No. 89)
Tuesday	Egg on Avocado (Page No. 45)	Tantalising Tuna & Spinach Mix (Page No. 54)	Chicken Avocado Creamy Salad (Page No. 84)
Wednesday	Keto egg muffins (Page No. 24)	Special Bacon Sandwich (Page No. 65)	Grilled Chicken Thighs Rosemary (Page No. 77)
Thursday	Anti-Inflammatory Spice Smoothie (Page No. 43)	Egg Medley Muffins (Page No. 51)	Keto Blueberry Kefir Smoothie (Page No. 88)
Friday	Bulletproof Coffee (Page No. 27)	Garlic Butter Chicken (Page No. 55)	Strawberries smoothie (Page No. 85)
Saturday	Chocolate Coconut Crunch Smoothie (Page No. 44)	Creamy Zucchini Noodles (Page No. 68)	Creamiest Chocolate Dessert (Page No. 91)

28-Days Keto Diet Weight Loss Challenge

Third-Week Meal Plan

Day	Breakfast	Lunch	Dinner
Sunday	Chocolate Coconut Crunch Smoothie (Page No. 44)	Creamy Zucchini Noodles (Page No. 60)	Creamiest Chocolate Dessert (Page No. 91)
Monday	Egg on Avocado (Page No. 45)	Tantalising Tuna & Spinach Mix (Page No. 54)	Chicken Avocado Creamy Salad (Page No. 84)
Tuesday	Keto egg muffins (Page No. 24)	Blueberry Smoothie (Page No. 58)	Grilled Chicken Thighs Rosemary (Page No. 77)
Wednesday	Bulletproof Coffee (Page No. 27)	Egg Medley Muffins (Page No. 51)	Keto Blueberry Kefir Smoothie (Page No. 88)
Thursday	Anti-Inflammatory Spice Smoothie (Page No. 43)	Creamy Zucchini Noodles (Page No. 68)	Crispy Almond Chicken with Tomato (Page No. 89)
Friday	Keto Coffee (Page No. 48)	Special Bacon Sandwich (Page No. 65)	Broccoli Cheddar Soup (Page No. 81)
Saturday	Egg & Sausage Breakfast (Page No. 23)	Coconut Chicken Curry (Page No. 50)	Crispy Chicken with Cheese Sauce (Page No. 82)

28-Days Keto Diet Weight Loss Challenge

Fourth Week Meal Plan

Day	Breakfast	Lunch	Dinner
Sunday	Perfect Strawberry Pancakes (Page No. 29)	Egg Medley Muffins (Page No. 51)	Keto Blueberry Kefir Smoothie (Page No. 88)
Monday	Bulletproof Coffee (Page No. 27)	Creamy Zucchini Noodles (Page No. 68)	Creamiest Chocolate Dessert (Page No. 91)
Tuesday	Blueberry Breakfast Smoothie (Page No. 33)	Garlic Butter Chicken (Page No. 55)	Strawberries smoothie (Page No. 85)
Wednesday	Egg & Sausage Breakfast (Page No. 23)	Mushrooms & Cream Cheese (Page No. 61)	Crispy Chicken with Cheese Sauce (Page No. 82)
Thursday	Egg on Avocado (Page No. 45)	Coconut Chicken Curry (Page No. 50)	Broccoli Cheddar Soup (Page No. 81)
Friday	Keto egg muffins (Page No. 24)	Tantalising Tuna & Spinach Mix (Page No. 54)	Chicken Avocado Creamy Salad (Page No. 84)
Saturday	Bulletproof Coffee (Page No. 27)	Blueberry Smoothie (Page No. 58)	Grilled Chicken Thighs Rosemary (Page No. 77)

Breakfast Recipes

Egg & Sausage Breakfast

TIME TO PREPARE

5 minutes

COOK TIME

45 minutes

SERVING

2 People

Nutrition per serving: Calories: 375, Protein: 21 g, Fat: 32 g, Net Carbs: 2 g

Ingredients	Instructions

Ingredients

- 12 eggs.
- 8 oz breakfast sausage.
- 8 oz cheddar cheese (grated).
- ¾ cup (180g) of thick cream or single cream.
- 1 tbsp onion (grated).
- 2 tsp mustard (powder).
- 1 tsp oregano (dried).

Instructions

1. Preheat oven to 350.
2. In a large frying pan, fry sausage for 6-7 minutes, breaking it with a fork as it cooks,
3. It eventually looks like a crumble mixture. Spread into a casserole dish.
4. In a bowl, mix eggs, cheese, onion, oregano, mustard, and cream until well
5. combined. Pour over the sausage mixture.
6. Bake for 35-40 minutes until thoroughly cooked.

Keto egg muffins

TIME TO PREPARE

10 minutes

COOK TIME

25 minutes

SERVING

1 People

Nutrition per serving: Calories: 336, Protein: 28 g, Fat: 70 g, Net Carbs: 2 g

Ingredients	Instructions
<ul><li>Two eggs</li><li>1/3 scallion, finely chopped</li><li>One slice of air-dried chorizo or salami or cooked bacon</li><li>2 Tbsp shredded cheese</li><li>1 tsp red pesto or green pesto (optional)</li><li>salt and pepper</li></ul>	1. Preheat the oven to 350°F (175°C). 2. Grease a muffin tin thoroughly with butter. 3. Chop scallions and chorizo and add to the bottom of the tin. 4. Whisk eggs together with seasoning and pesto. Add the cheese and stir. 5. Pour the batter on top of the scallions and chorizo. 6. Bake for 15–20 minutes, depending on the muffin tin size.

Bacon & Broccoli Wrap

TIME TO PREPARE

05 minutes

SERVING

2 People

COOK TIME

05 minutes

Nutrition per serving: Calories: 258, Protein: 15 g, Fat: 19 g, Net Carbs: 9 g

Ingredients

- One large egg.
- One cup (150g) broccoli (chopped).
- One onion (sliced).
- One slice of bacon.
- ¼ cup (50g) tomatoes (chopped).
- 2 tbsp cheddar cheese.
- 1 tbsp milk.
- 1 tsp avocado oil.
- Pinch salt and pepper

Instructions

1. Fry bacon until crispy and remove from pan. Add broccoli and cook for 3 minutes until soft; mix in tomatoes and pour into a bowl.
2. mix egg, milk, onion, salt and pepper in a separate bowl. Add oil to a large frying
3. pan over medium heat; pour in the egg mixture, covering the frying pan's base. Cook for 2 minutes until the bottom has set; flip it, and cook the other side.
4. Place an egg wrap on a plate, fill the bottom half with a broccoli mixture, top with bacon, and roll it into a wrap.

Avocado Coconut Milk Shake

TIME TO PREPARE

5 minutes

COOK TIME

0 minutes

SERVING

1 People

Nutrition per serving: Calories: 258, Protein: 15 g, Fat: 19 g, Net Carbs: 9 g

Ingredients	Instructions

Ingredients

- ½ avocado
- ½ cups (120g) Unsweetened Coconut Milk
- 5 drops stevia
- 5 Ice Cubes

Instructions

1. Add all the ingredients to the blender.
2. Blend until smooth.

Bulletproof Coffee

TIME TO PREPARE

5 minutes

SERVING

1 People

COOK TIME

10 minutes

Nutrition per serving: Calories: 224, Protein: 16 g, Fat: 44 g, Net Carbs: 0.12 g

Ingredients	Instructions

Ingredients

- 1 cup (250g) of water
- 2 tbsp coffee
- 1 tbsp grass-fed butter
- 1 tbsp coconut oil
- ¼ tsp vanilla extract

Instructions

1. Brew coffee your preferred way.
2. Add butter and coconut oil to the blender.
3. Pour the coffee into the blender.
4. Add the vanilla extract and blend for 20 seconds.

Cinnamon Chia Pudding

TIME TO PREPARE

5 minutes

COOK TIME

0 minutes

SERVING

1 People

Nutrition per serving: Calories: 384, Protein: 16 g, Fat: 24 g, Net Carbs: 10 g

Ingredients	Instructions

Ingredients

- 1 tbsp chia seeds
- 1 cup (240ml) unsweetened almond milk
- ½ tsp ground cinnamon
- 1 tbsp peanut butter
- 8 drops stevia

Instructions

1. Add almond milk, peanut butter, cinnamon, and stevia to your blender.
2. Blend until smooth.
3. Add chia seeds to the mixture and stir.
4. Refrigerate for about 3 hours.
5. Enjoy!

Perfect Strawberry Pancakes

TIME TO PREPARE

05 minutes

COOK TIME

15 minutes

SERVING

4 People

Nutrition per serving: Calories: 324, Protein: 14 g, Fat: 40 g, Net Carbs: 4 g

Ingredients	Instructions

Ingredients

- Four large eggs.
- 1 cup (240g) of thick cream or single cream.
- 7 oz cottage cheese.
- 2 oz fresh strawberries.
- 2 oz butter.

  1 tbsp psyllium husk (powder).

Instructions

1. Mix cottage cheese, eggs, and psyllium husk until well combined. Allow resting for 10 minutes.
2. Heat butter in a large frying pan and fry each pancake on medium heat for 3-4 minutes on each side.
3. In a bowl, whip the cream until peaks are formed.
4. Serve the pancakes topped with cream and fresh strawberries.

Mixed Berry & Coconut Porridge

TIME TO PREPARE

10 minutes

COOK TIME

00 minutes

SERVING

2 People

Nutrition per serving: Calories: 444, Protein: 10 g, Fat: 40 g, Net Carbs: 6 g

Ingredients	Instructions
<ul><li>½ cup (120g) almond milk.</li><li>¼ cup (70g) of mixed berries.</li><li>⅓ cup (80ml) of coconut milk.</li><li>2 tbsp flaxseed.</li><li>1 tbsp desiccated coconut.</li><li>1 tbsp almond meal.</li><li>1 tsp pumpkin seeds.</li><li>½ tsp cinnamon.</li><li>½ tsp vanilla extract.</li></ul>	1. To a large saucepan, add coconut milk, almond milk, flaxseed, almond meal, coconut, cinnamon, and vanilla; stir continuously until the mixture thickens. 2. Pour into a bowl and top with pumpkin seeds and mixed fruit.

Egg & Bacon Bakes

TIME TO PREPARE

5 minutes

COOK TIME

15 minutes

SERVING

4 People

Nutrition per serving: Calories: 296, Protein: 16 g, Fat: 25 g, Net Carbs: 2 g

Ingredients	Instructions

- Six large eggs.
- Six bacon slices (chopped).
- 1 ½ cups (170g) cheddar cheese (grated).
- 6 tbsp salsa.
- 1 tbsp olive oil.
- 1 tsp black pepper.
- 1 tsp chilli flakes.
- 1 tsp paprika.
- ½ tsp salt.

1. Preheat the oven to 400 and line a baking sheet with greaseproof paper.
2. Split the cheese into six piles on the baking sheet.
3. Season the piles with paprika and chilli flakes and bake for 10-11 minutes.
4. Place each cheese bake over an upside-down cup; allow it to cool and mould itself to the shape. Set aside.
5. Heat the oil in a frying pan and fry the bacon until crispy. Remove bacon from the pan, but leave the grease in the pan.
6. Heat the bacon grease, scramble six eggs, season with salt and pepper, and add to the cheese bakes.
7. Top each with 1 tbsp salsa and sprinkle each with bacon.

Stuffed Bacon Boats

TIME TO PREPARE

10 minutes

COOK TIME

30 minutes

SERVING

8 boats

Nutrition per serving: Calories: 468, Protein: 19 g, Fat: 42 g, Net Carbs: 3 g

Ingredients

- 18 bacon slices.
- Seven large eggs.
- 1 ½ cups (170g) cheddar cheese.
- 4 tbsp thick cream.
- ½ tsp black pepper.
- ½ tsp onion powder.
- ½ tsp paprika.

Instructions

1. Preheat oven to 375.
2. line each hole with bacon slices in a large muffin tray, ensuring no gaps at the bottom or sides. Bake for 15 minutes.
3. whisk eggs, cream, black pepper, onion powder, and paprika in a large bowl.
4. spoon 2 tbsp of cheese in each bacon cup and top with egg mixture.
5. Bake for 15 minutes until eggs are thoroughly cooked and turning golden brown.

Blueberry Breakfast Smoothie

TIME TO PREPARE

5 minutes

COOK TIME

0 minutes

SERVING

1 People

Nutrition per serving: Calories: 293, Protein: 5 g, Fat: 27 g, Net Carbs: 6 g

Ingredients	Instructions

- ½ cup (70g) ice (crushed).
- ½ cup (120g) of thick cream or single cream.
- ½ cup (90g) blueberries.
- 3 tbsp Greek yoghurt (total fat).

  1 ½ tbsp macadamia oil.

1. Put iall iingredients iinto ia iblender iuntil ithick iand icreamy.

Tasty Turkey Rolls

TIME TO PREPARE

05 minutes

COOK TIME

10 minutes

SERVING

1 People

Nutrition per serving: Calories: 216, Protein: 18 g, Fat: 15 g, Net Carbs: 1 g

Ingredients	Instructions

Ingredients

- One turkey slice.
- One large egg.
- 2 tbsp cheddar cheese (grated).
- 1 tsp mixed herbs (chopped).

  Cooking spray.

Instructions

1. Spray a frying pan with cooking spray and heat it to medium.
2. Mix egg and herbs and pour into a hot frying pan.
3. Swirl the mixture around the pan until all of the pan is coated.
4. flip the egg and add cheese when the bottom is firm.
5. When completely cooked through, remove from the pan and line the turkey slice in the middle; roll it into a sausage shape.

Pumpkin Pots

TIME TO PREPARE

05 minutes

COOK TIME

10 minutes

SERVING

1 People

Nutrition per serving: Calories: 239, Protein: 13 g, Fat: 17 g, Net Carbs: 4 g

Ingredients	Instructions

Ingredients

- One large egg.
- 2 tbsp swerve.
- 2 tbsp flaxseed.
- 2 tbsp pumpkin puree.
- 2 tbsp almond flour.
- 1 ½ tsp pumpkin spice.
- ¼ tsp baking powder.

  Cooking spray.

Instructions

1. Spray a small ramekin with cooking spray and crack in egg and pumpkin puree; mix until well combined.
2. In a bowl, mix swerve, flaxseed, almond flour, pumpkin spice, and baking powder until well combined; add to egg mixture.
3. Microwave on high for 1 ½ minutes until thoroughly cooked.
4. Let stand for 1 minute.

Keto Zucchini (courgette) Boats

TIME TO PREPARE

10 minutes

COOK TIME

30 minutes

SERVING

4 People

Nutrition per serving: Calories: 166, Protein: 11 g, Fat: 13 g, Net Carbs: 2 g

Ingredients	Instructions
<ul><li>3 Zucchini or courgette</li><li>100g (1 Cup) precut Bacon</li><li>50g (3Tbsp) Cream Cheese</li><li>100g (1cup) Blue Cheese</li><li>100g (1 Cup) Gouda Cheese</li><li>4 basil leaves cut</li><li>Salt & pepper</li></ul>	1. Preheat the oven to 190C or 370F 2. Wash and Cut Zucchini. 3. Cut each of the zucchinis diagonally halfway through. 4. With a spoon or knife, clean the inside of both sides. 5. Place all the fillings per the recipe into a big bowl and adequately mix them. 6. Fill each half of the Zucchini fully and place them onto a baking sheet covered with Parchment Paper. 7. Place the Filled Zucchini into the oven and bake thoroughly for 30 minutes

Coconut Chai Smoothie

TIME TO PREPARE

10 minutes

COOK TIME

00 minutes

SERVING

1 People

Nutrition per serving: Calories: 473, Protein: 25 g, Fat: 38 g, Net Carbs: 4 g

Ingredients	Instructions

- ⅓ cup (60g) coconut cream
- 2 tbsp. low-carb plain or vanilla protein powder
- 1 tbsp. MCT oil
- ¼ tsp. each cinnamon and ginger
- pinch cardamom and nutmeg
- dash vanilla extract

  ½ cup strong black tea, chilled

1. Blend all ingredients until smooth. Add water to reach the desired consistency.

Keto Chocolate Chip Cookies

TIME TO PREPARE

5 minutes

COOK TIME

15 minutes

SERVING

10 Cookies

Nutrition per serving: Calories: 132, Protein: 3 g, Fat: 11 g, Net Carbs: 1 g

Ingredients	Instructions

Ingredients

- 100 g / 1 cup almond flour
- 1 medium egg
- 2 tbsp heavy cream
- 2 tbsp butter unsalted, VERY soft
- 3 tbsp granulated sweetener
- 1 tsp vanilla extract
- 50 g dark chocolate/chocolate chips (sugar-free)

Instructions

1. Preheat the oven to 180 Celsius/356 Fahrenheit
2. Combine all ingredients apart from the chocolate with a fork. Let the dough sit for a few minutes so the flour can absorb the moisture
3. Chop your chocolate and stir into the dough
4. Form dough balls with your hand or spoon the mixture on a baking sheet lined with baking paper. Press down into the desired shape (ca ½ cm thick)
5. Bake for about 13 minutes or until the edges are nicely browned. They are soft when straight out of the oven but firm up as they cool down.

Egg & Goats Cheese

TIME TO PREPARE

05 minutes

COOK TIME

5 minutes

SERVING

4 People

Nutrition per serving: Calories: 249, Protein: 15 g, Fat: 10 g, Net Carbs: 2 g

Ingredients	Instructions

Ingredients

- Eight large eggs.
- One tomato (chopped).
- 2 oz goat's cheese.
- 2 tbsp water.
- ¼ cup (40g) of mixed fresh herbs (chopped).
- 1 tbsp butter.
- ½ tsp salt.
  ¼ tsp black pepper

Instructions

1. Whisk together eggs, salt, pepper, and water.
2. Heat butter in a large frying pan, add egg mixture, and scramble for 2-3 minutes until cooked; blend in tomatoes and remove from heat.
3. Fold in goat's cheese and herbs.

Egg & Bacon Sandwich

TIME TO PREPARE

05 minutes

COOK TIME

15 minutes

SERVING

1 People

Nutrition per serving: Calories: 594, Protein: 19 g, Fat: 54 g, Net Carbs: 7 g

Ingredients	Instructions

Ingredients

- 2 slices Keto Bread
- 2 teaspoons Butter
- 1 tablespoon Keto Pepper Relish
- 2 ounces Bacon
- 1 large Egg
- Pinch Salt

  Pinch Pepper

Instructions

1. Butter both sides of the Keto Bread.
2. Place the bread into a non-stick pan over medium heat and toast each side for 2-3 minutes, until golden brown. Set aside on a plate and spread with the Keto Pepper Relish.
3. Add the bacon to the pan and increase to high heat. Cook the bacon to your desired crispiness and add to the toasted bread.
4. Fry the egg in the bacon grease to your desired doneness and place on top of the bacon.
5. Sprinkle with salt and pepper, then top with the second piece of toast and enjoy

Chorizo & Egg Breakfast

TIME TO PREPARE

05 minutes

COOK TIME

30 minutes

SERVING

4 People

Nutrition per serving: Calories: 335, Protein: 23 g, Fat: 27 g, Net Carbs: 2 g

Ingredients	Instructions

Ingredients

- 10 eggs.
- 6 oz cheddar cheese (grated).
- 5 oz chorizo (chopped).
- Two spring onions (chopped).
- Salt and pepper.
- Cooking spray.

Instructions

1. Preheat the oven to 350 and grease a large muffin tray.
2. Add the onions and chorizo to the bottom of each muffin tray hole.
3. Whisk together eggs, cheese, salt, and pepper; pour on top of the onions and chorizo.
4. Bake for 20-25 minutes until cooked through

Keto Bread Recipe

TIME TO PREPARE

10 minutes

COOK TIME

30 minutes

SERVING

16 Slice

Nutrition per serving: Calories: 140, Protein: 3 g, Fat: 13 g, Net Carbs: 3 g

Ingredients

- 2 tsp Dry Yeast
- 1 tsp Inulin
- 2 tbsp Warm Water
- 7.5 oz Almond Flour
- 1 tbsp Psyllium Husk Powder
- 1 tsp Baking Powder
- 1/2 tsp Xanthan Gum
- 1 pinch Salt
- 4.5 oz Unsalted Butter melted
- 7 large Eggs

Instructions

1. Preheat your oven to 170C/340F.
2. Add the yeast and inulin to a small mixing bowl, followed by the warm water. Mix well and leave to proof in a warm place for 10 minutes.
3. In a large mixing bowl, add the almond flour, psyllium, baking powder, xanthan gum, and salt. Mix well.
4. Add the melted butter and eggs and mix well.
5. Add the proofed yeast and mix well.
6. Once the mixture is combined, pour it into a 9x5in loaf pan lined with parchment paper.
7. Leave your batter to dry for 20 minutes in a warm spot, covered with a tea towel.
8. Bake in the oven for 30-40 minutes; the bread is cooked when golden brown and makes a hollow sound when tapped.
9. Remove from the tin and leave to cool on a rack.

Anti-Inflammatory Spice Smoothie

TIME TO PREPARE

05 minutes

COOK TIME

0 minutes

SERVING

1 People

Nutrition per serving: Calories: 601.2, Protein: 25 g, Fat: 49.5 g, Net Carbs: 8 g

Ingredients	Instructions

- 6 ounces. Ground beef
- 4 eggs
- 4 ounces. shredded cheese

1. Blend all ingredients until smooth.

Chocolate Coconut Crunch Smoothie

TIME TO PREPARE

5 minutes

COOK TIME

0 minutes

SERVING

1 People

Nutrition per serving: Calories: 633.5, Protein: 31.1 g, Fat: 53.9 g, Net Carbs: 6 g

Ingredients	Instructions

Ingredients

- One avocado
- 2 tbsp. low-carb chocolate protein powder
- 1 tbsp. MCT oil
- water
- 2 tbsp. chopped almonds

  2 tbsp. Unsweetened coconut flakes

Instructions

1. Blend the avocado, protein powder, MCT oil, and water until smooth. Stir in the almonds and coconut flakes and serve.

Egg Baked in Avocado

TIME TO PREPARE

10 minutes

COOK TIME

15 minutes

SERVING

4 People

Nutrition per serving: Calories: 261.4, Protein: 14.5 g, Fat: 20.9 g, Net Carbs: 4 g

Ingredients	Instructions

Ingredients

- One teaspoon of garlic powder
- 1/2 teaspoon sea salt
- 1/4 cup (30g) Parmesan cheese
- 1/4 teaspoon black pepper
- Three medium avocados
- Six medium eggs

Instructions

1. Prepare muffin tins and preheat oven to 350oF.
2. To ensure the egg would fit inside the avocado's cavity, lightly scrape off 1/3 of the meat.
3. Place avocado on a muffin tin to ensure it faces the top-up.
4. Evenly season each avocado with pepper, salt, and garlic powder.
5. Add one egg to each avocado cavity and garnish tops with cheese.
6. Pop in the oven and bake until the egg white is set, around 15 minutes.
7. Serve and enjoy.

Keto Starbucks Egg Bites

TIME TO PREPARE

05 minutes

SERVING

6 egg bites

COOK TIME

30 minutes

Nutrition per serving: Calories: 137, Protein: 11 g, Fat: 10.5 g, Net Carbs: 0.6 g

Ingredients	Instructions

Ingredients

- 10 eggs
- 1 cup (112g) shredded gruyere, swiss, or cheddar
- 1/2 cup (75g) whole-fat cottage cheese or cream cheese
- ¼ teaspoon kosher salt
- Couple cracks of fresh black pepper

  4-5 slices of sugar-free bacon

Instructions

1. Make sure to cook the slices of bacon before making the egg bites. Preheat oven to 350 degrees F and place a baking dish filled with 1 inch of water on the bottom rack. This will create a humid environment and help the eggs cook evenly. Add the eggs, cheese, cottage cheese, salt, and pepper to a blender and blend on high for 20 seconds until light and frothy. Spray a muffin tin with a little non-stick spray and fill the tins almost to the top with the egg mixture. Divide the chopped bacon equally among the muffin tins and bake in the oven for 30 minutes, or until the centre of the egg bites is set. Remove from oven and let cool for 5 minutes, then use a spatula or fork to remove them from the muffin tin carefully. Enjoy!

Healthy Breakfast Granola

TIME TO PREPARE

05 minutes

COOK TIME

15 minutes

SERVING

4 People

Nutrition per serving: Calories: 458.2, Protein: 11.4 g, Fat: 42.7 g, Net Carbs: 11 g

Ingredients	Instructions

Ingredients

- 1 cup (120g) walnuts, diced
- 1 cup (120g) unsweetened coconut flakes
- Two tablespoons of coconut oil, melted
- Four packets of Splenda
- Two teaspoons of cinnamon

Instructions

1. Preheat the oven to 375 F / 190 C.
2. Spray a baking tray with cooking spray and set aside.
3. Add all ingredients into the medium bowl and toss well.
4. Spread the bowl mixture on a baking tray and bake in a preheated oven for 10 minutes.
5. Serve and enjoy.

Keto Coffee

TIME TO PREPARE

10 minutes

COOK TIME

00 minutes

SERVING

2 People

Nutrition per serving: Calories: 260.2, Protein: 1 g, Fat: 26.2 g, Net Carbs: 0 g

Ingredients	Instructions

Ingredients

- 1 cup (10g) of black coffee (brewed)
- 1 tbsp. of butter
- 1/2 tbsp. of coconut oil
- One teaspoon of cinnamon

Instructions

1. Brew black coffee.
2. combine coconut oil, coffee, and butter in a blender.
3. Blend well. Add cinnamon or stevia, and serve!

Keto Lunch Recipes

Garlic Chicken with Cauliflower Mash

TIME TO PREPARE

10 minutes

COOK TIME

50 minutes

SERVING

4 People

Nutrition per serving: Calories: 694, Protein: 48.5 g, Fat: 49.1 g, Net Carbs: 11 g

Ingredients	Instructions

Cauliflower mash:

- One large cauliflower head (chopped).
- One cup (100g) of chicken stock.
- 3 tbsp butter (cubed).
- 1 tsp salt.
- 1 tsp fresh thyme (chopped).

Garlic chicken:

- 32 oz chicken drumsticks.
- Six garlic cloves (finely chopped).
- ½ cup (40g) fresh parsley (chopped).
- 2 oz butter.
- Juice of 1 lemon.
- 2 tbsp olive oil.

1. Preheat oven to 450 degrees.
2. Place the chicken in a greased ovenproof dish.
3. Drizzle olive oil and lemon juice on the chicken and top with garlic and parsley.
4. Bake for 40-45 minutes or until chicken is thoroughly cooked and browned. Cauliflower mash:
5. bring chicken stock and salt to boil in a large pan.
6. Add cauliflower, bring it back to boil, reduce heat, and simmer for 15-20 minutes or until cauliflower is tender.
7. Take cauliflower from the pan and add to a blender with 3 tbsp of the stock.
8. Add the butter and thyme; blend until smooth and well combined.

Coconut Chicken Curry

TIME TO PREPARE

10 minutes

SERVING

4 People

COOK TIME

30 minutes

Nutrition per serving: Calories: 1190, Protein: 32 g, Fat: 112 g, Net Carbs: 12 g

Ingredients	Instructions

Ingredients

- 27 oz coconut milk.
- 16 oz chicken thighs
- 8 oz broccoli (cut into small florets).
- 3 oz green beans (cut in half).
- One onion (finely chopped).
- One chili pepper (finely chopped).
- 3 tbsp coconut oil.
- 1 tbsp fresh ginger.
- 1 tbsp curry paste.
- Salt and Pepper.

Cauliflower rice:

- 24 oz cauliflower head (grated).
- 3 oz coconut oil.
- ½ tsp salt.

Instructions

1. Heat coconut oil in a frying pan. Add onion, chili, and ginger and fry until softened.
2. Add chicken and curry paste; fry until chicken is cooked and lightly browned.
3. Add broccoli and green beans.
4. Add a substantial part of coconut milk, salt, and Pepper. Allow simmering for 15-20 minutes.
5. In another large frying pan, add 3 oz coconut oil. When hot, add the grated cauliflower.
6. Add salt and cook for 5-10 minutes until rice has softened.
7. Place rice on a serving plate and top with chicken curry.

Egg Medley Muffins

TIME TO PREPARE

05 minutes

COOK TIME

35 minutes

SERVING

4 People

Nutrition per serving: Calories: 332, Protein: 22.5 g, Fat: 28 g, Net Carbs: 2 g

Ingredients	Instructions

Ingredients

- 12 large eggs.
- One onion (finely chopped).
- 6 oz cheddar cheese (grated).
- 5 oz bacon (cooked and diced).
- Pinch salt and pepper.

Instructions

1. Preheat the oven to 175 degrees and grease a 12-hole muffin tray.
2. Equally, place onion and bacon at the bottom of each muffin tray hole.
3. whisk the eggs, cheese, salt, and pepper in a large bowl.
4. Pour the egg mixture into each hole on the onions and bacon.
5. Bake for 20-25 minutes, until browned and firm to the touch.

Keto Stuffed Mushrooms

TIME TO PREPARE

10 minutes

COOK TIME

25 minutes

SERVING

4 People

Nutrition per serving: Calories: 140, Protein: 8 g, Fat: 7 g, Net Carbs: 3 g

Ingredients	Instructions

Ingredients

- 12 small mushrooms
- 1 cup (156g) frozen spinach thawed and drained
- 1 cup (225g) shredded mozzarella divided
- 4 oz cream cheese softened
- 8 sundried tomatoes chopped
- 1 teaspoon garlic powder

  ½ teaspoon salt

Instructions

1. Preheat oven to 400.
2. Remove stems from the mushrooms and discard or save them for another use.
3. Stir together half the mozzarella and the other ingredients. Divide between the mushrooms. They will overflow, but the filling shrinks. Sprinkle with the rest of the mozzarella.
4. Bake for 20-25 minutes. Until the mushrooms have softened and the cheese is golden.

Speedy roast chicken

TIME TO PREPARE

15 minutes

COOK TIME

60 minutes

SERVING

4 People

Nutrition per serving: Calories: 188.5, Protein: 15 g, Fat: 12.3 g, Net Carbs: 4 g

Ingredients	Instructions

Ingredients

- 1 whole chicken
- 1 tablespoon olive oil
- 1/4 teaspoon salt
- 1/4 teaspoon ground black pepper
- 1/4 teaspoon dried oregano
- 1/4 teaspoon dried basil
- 1/4 teaspoon paprika
- 1/8 teaspoon cayenne pepper

Instructions

1. Preheat oven to 230 C / Gas 8.
2. Put the chicken into a small roasting tin. Rub with olive oil. Mix the spices and rub into the chicken.
3. Roast the chicken in the preheated oven for 20 minutes. Lower the oven temperature to 200 C / Gas mark 6 and continue roasting for 40 minutes to a minimum internal temperature of 85 C. Remove from oven and let sit 10 to 15 minutes, and serve.

Tantalising Tuna & Spinach Mix

TIME TO PREPARE

5 minutes

SERVING

2 People

COOK TIME

15 minutes

Nutrition per serving: Calories: 953, Protein: 53 g, Fat: 80.3 g, Net Carbs: 3.1 g

Ingredients	Instructions

Ingredients

- Four large eggs.
- 10 oz tinned tuna (in olive oil).
- ½ cup (120g) mayonnaise.
- One avocado (sliced).
- One onion (finely diced).

  Salt and pepper (to season).

Instructions

1. Bring a large pan of water to a boil and lower in the eggs. Cook for 8 minutes.
2. mix tuna, mayonnaise, onion, salt, and pepper in a bowl.
3. Chop the hard-boiled eggs into halves and place them on a plate with avocado slices and spinach.
4. Place the tuna mixture on top of the spinach.

Garlic Butter Chicken

TIME TO PREPARE

10 minutes

COOK TIME

30 minutes

SERVING

4 People

Nutrition per serving: Calories: 899, Protein: 62 g, Fat: 72.1 g, Net Carbs: 2 g

Ingredients	Instructions

Ingredients

- Four chicken breasts (defrosted).
- 6 oz butter (room temperature).
- One garlic clove (crushed).
- 3 tbsp olive oil.
- 1 tsp lemon juice.
- ½ tsp salt.
- ½ tsp garlic powder.

Instructions

1. Mix butter, garlic powder, garlic clove, lemon juice, and salt. When well combined, set aside.
2. Heat the oil in a large frying pan and fry chicken breasts until thoroughly cooked and golden brown.
3. Place chicken on a plate and smoothly smother each chicken breast with garlic butter mixture.

Coconut Keto Chicken Curry

TIME TO PREPARE

10 minutes

COOK TIME

30 minutes

SERVING

4 People

Nutrition per serving: Calories: 374, Protein: 34 g, Fat: 27.1 g, Net Carbs: 2 g

Ingredients	Instructions

Ingredients

- 24 oz chicken thighs (lean & defrosted).
- One ¼ cup (360g) coconut milk.
- ⅓ cup (50g) red onion (diced).
- 4 tsp curry paste.
- Cooking spray.

Instructions

1. Preheat the oven to 200 degrees.
2. Rub chicken with 2 tsp of curry paste. Set aside for 20-25 minutes.
3. Spray a large frying pan with cooking spray, fry onions and add in the remaining 2 tsp curry paste and fry for 3-4 minutes.
4. Place chicken thighs in the pan with onions and sear for 3-4 minutes. Turn the chicken over, reduce heat, and pour in coconut milk. Simmer for 7-8 minutes.
5. Pour the curry mixture into a large ovenproof dish and bake for 15-20 minutes.

Broccoli Cheese Baked Bites

TIME TO PREPARE

10 minutes

COOK TIME

35 minutes

SERVING

24 bites

Nutrition per serving: Calories: 61, Protein: 6 g, Fat: 6 g, Net Carbs: 1 g

Ingredients	Instructions

Ingredients

- Two cups (170g) broccoli (florets).
- Two eggs.
- One cup (120g) cheddar cheese (grated).
- ½ cup (70g) spinach.
- ¼ cup (38g) onions (diced).
- ¼ cup (25g) parmesan (grated).
- ⅓ cup (60g) sour cream.
- One lemon zest.

Instructions

1. Preheat the oven to 180 degrees.
2. Place broccoli in a microwave-safe bowl with ¼ cup of water. Microwave for 3 minutes on high or until broccoli is tender.
3. Chop broccoli florets into small pieces and place in a large bowl. Add all other ingredients and mix well until thoroughly combined.
4. Line an ovenproof dish with greaseproof paper and pour in the mixture.
5. Bake for 25-30 minutes until puffed and browned.
6. Cool for 10 minutes and cut into 24 square bites.

Blueberry Smoothie

TIME TO PREPARE

5 minutes

COOK TIME

0 minutes

SERVING

2 People

Nutrition per serving: Calories: 257, Protein: 10 g, Fat: 20 g, Net Carbs: 5 g

Ingredients	Instructions

Ingredients

- 1 large avocado
- 1/2 cup (10g) frozen blueberries
- 4 tsp flax seeds
- 2 tbsp collagen powder
- 1 1/2 cups (350 ml) of almond milk

Instructions

1. Put all the ingredients into a blender and blend until smooth.

Buttered Cabbage Stir Fry

TIME TO PREPARE

05 minutes

COOK TIME

20 minutes

SERVING

1 People

Nutrition per serving: Calories: 380, Protein: 4 g, Fat: 43 g, Net Carbs: 3 g

Ingredients	Instructions

- 5 oz cabbage (cut into long strips).
- 2 oz butter.
- Two bacon slices (diced).

1. In a large frying pan, melt half of the butter and fry the bacon until crispy.
2. Add the remaining butter and stir in the cabbage; cook until the cabbage changes colour.

Bacon & Spinach Bake

TIME TO PREPARE

10 minutes

COOK TIME

35 minutes

SERVING

4 People

Nutrition per serving: Calories: 660, Protein: 28.2 g, Fat: 61.5 g, Net Carbs: 4 g

Ingredients	Instructions

Ingredients

- Eight large eggs.
- 8 oz fresh spinach.
- One cup (240g) of thick or single cream.
- 5 oz bacon (diced).
- 5 oz cheddar cheese (grated).
- 2 tbsp butter.

Instructions

1. Preheat the oven to 175 degrees.
2. In a large frying pan, melt the butter and fry the bacon until crispy. Add in the spinach and fry until wilted. Set aside.
3. In a large bowl, whisk together the eggs and cream.
4. Pour the egg mixture into an ovenproof dish; add bacon and spinach, and top with cheese.
5. Bake for 25-30 minutes until completely set and golden brown.

Mushrooms & Cream Cheese

TIME TO PREPARE

05 minutes

SERVING

4 People

COOK TIME

30 minutes

Nutrition per serving: Calories: 475, Protein: 13.2 g, Fat: 47.5 g, Net Carbs: 5 g

Ingredients	Instructions

Ingredients

- 12 mushrooms.
- 8 oz bacon.
- 7 oz cream cheese.
- 3 tbsp fresh chives (finely diced).
- 1 tbsp butter.
- 1 tsp paprika.
- ½ tsp chilli flakes.

Instructions

1. Preheat the oven to 200 degrees.
2. In a frying pan, cook the bacon until crispy; remove the bacon, leaving the pan fat. Allow bacon to cool, then crumble until it resembles large breadcrumbs.
3. Remove stems from the mushrooms and finely chop. Add a little butter to the bacon fat and saute the mushroom cups.
4. mix cream cheese, bacon, chopped mushroom stems, chives, and paprika until well combined.
5. Divide the mixture evenly into each mushroom cup; place on a baking tray and bake for 20-25 minutes or until golden brown.
6. Sprinkle chilli flakes on top.

Bacon, Cheese & Herb Balls

TIME TO PREPARE

10 minutes

COOK TIME

25 minutes

SERVING

8 balls

Nutrition per serving: Calories: 273, Protein: 9 g, Fat: 29.5 g, Net Carbs: 2 g

Ingredients	Instructions

Ingredients

- 5 oz cheddar cheese (grated).
- 5 oz cream cheese.
- 5 oz bacon.
- 2 oz butter.
- ½ tsp chilli flakes.
- ½ tsp black pepper.
- ½ tsp Italian seasoning.

Instructions

1. Heat the butter in a large pan and fry the bacon until crispy. Reserve bacon fat and chop the bacon into small pieces.
2. mix cream cheese, cheddar cheese, chilli flakes, pepper, Italian seasoning, and bacon fat until well combined.
3. Place the cream cheese mix in the fridge for 20 minutes.
4. When the mixture is set, roll 24 balls into shape.
5. Roll each ball in the bacon pieces before serving.

Smoked Salmon Lettuce Wrap

TIME TO PREPARE

10 minutes

COOK TIME

25 minutes

SERVING

4 People

Nutrition per serving: Calories: 263, Protein: 10 g, Fat: 24.1 g, Net Carbs: 3 g

Ingredients

- 8 oz cream cheese
- 7 oz smoked salmon (canned and drained).
- 2 oz iceberg lettuce leaves.
- 5 tbsp mayonnaise.
- 4 tbsp chives (finely chopped).
- ½ lemon zest.

Instructions

1. mix everything (except lettuce leaves) in a large bowl until well combined.
2. Place in the refrigerator for 15-20 minutes.
3. When chilled, scoop onto lettuce leaves and serve.

Keto Green Smoothie

TIME TO PREPARE

10 minutes

SERVING

2 People

COOK TIME

30 minutes

Nutrition per serving: Calories: 381, Protein: 12 g, Fat: 36 g, Net Carbs: 5 g

Ingredients

Instructions

- 2 cups (60 g) spinach
- 1/3 cup (46 g) raw almonds
- 2 Brazil nuts
- 1 cup (240 ml) coconut milk
- 1 Tablespoon (10 g) psyllium seeds (or psyllium husks) or chia seeds

1. Place the spinach, almonds, Brazil nuts, and coconut milk into the blender.
2. Blend until pureed.
3. Add the ingredients (greens powder, psyllium seeds) and blend well.

Special Bacon Sandwich

TIME TO PREPARE

05 minutes

COOK TIME

20 minutes

SERVING

1 People

Nutrition per serving: Calories: 490, Protein: 28 g, Fat: 39 g, Net Carbs: 6 g

Ingredients	Instructions

Ingredients

- Cooking spray.
- Two large eggs.
- 1 tbsp coconut flour.
- 1 tbsp butter (salted).
- ¼ tsp baking powder.
- One slice of cheddar cheese.
- Two slices of bacon (grilled)

Instructions

1. Place butter in the microwave for 30 seconds or until melted.
2. Let the butter cool slightly. Mix in 1 egg, coconut flour, and baking powder; microwave for one and a half minutes.
3. Allow bread to cool and slice to make two equally thin slices.
4. Using the cooking spray, fry the remaining egg to your preference. Grill the bread until toasted and crunchy.
5. Assemble the sandwich, placing a slice of toast on the bottom, cheese, bacon, fried egg, and top with the remaining toast.

Pesto Egg Muffins

TIME TO PREPARE

10 minutes

COOK TIME

30 minutes

SERVING

10 muffins

Nutrition per serving: Calories: 252, Protein: 13 g, Fat: 20 g, Net Carbs: 2 g

Ingredients	Instructions

Ingredients

- 2/3 cup (100g) frozen spinach, thawed and excess water removed
- 3 tbsp pesto (45g) - you can make your pesto
- 1/2 cup (50g) kalamata or other olives, pitted
- 1/4 cup (28g) sun-dried tomatoes, chopped
- 125 g soft goat cheese
- 6 large eggs
- sea salt and black pepper to taste

Instructions

1. Preheat the oven to 175 °C/ 350 °F (fan assisted), or 195 °C/ 380 °F (conventional). Squeeze out the excess water from the spinach, deseed, slice the olives, and chop the sun-dried tomatoes. Crack the eggs into a bowl.
2. Add the pesto and season with salt and pepper to taste. Mix until well combined.
3. Divide the spinach, crumbled goat cheese, sun-dried tomatoes and olives evenly into a medium-large silicon muffin pan. (If using a regular pan, lightly grease with olive oil or ghee.)
4. Pour in the egg & pesto mixture and transfer into the oven. Bake for 20 to 25 minutes or until browned on top and cooked inside.
5. When done, remove it from the oven and set it aside to cool down. Store in the fridge for up to 5 days. Freeze for up to 3 months.

Keto Tuna Salad

TIME TO PREPARE

5 minutes

COOK TIME

0 minutes

SERVING

4 People

Nutrition per serving: Calories: 225, Protein: 13 g, Fat: 16 g, Net Carbs: 3 g

Ingredients	Instructions

Ingredients

- 10 oz. (280g) canned tuna (drained)
- 1 large avocado
- 1 celery rib
- 2 cloves fresh garlic
- 3 tablespoon mayonnaise
- 1 small red onion
- 1 tablespoon freshly squeezed lemon juice
- 1/4 cucumber
- 1 handful parsley
- 1/4 teaspoon salt

  pepper to taste

Instructions

1. Rinse and dry the vegetables. Finely chop the cucumber, onion, and celery. Mince the garlic.
2. Set aside half of the parsley, then add the rest of the ingredients to a large bowl.
3. Mix everything until the avocado is well-mashed and all the ingredients have been coated. Add salt and pepper to taste.
4. Garnish with remaining parsley before serving.

Creamy Zucchini Noodles

TIME TO PREPARE

10 minutes

COOK TIME

25 minutes

SERVING

2 People

Nutrition per serving: Calories: 801, Protein: 21.2 g, Fat: 78 g, Net Carbs: 7 g

Ingredients	Instructions

Ingredients

- 32 oz zucchini or courgette.
- 10 oz bacon (diced).
- One ¼ cup (300g) thick or single cream.
- ¼ cup mayonnaise.
- 3 oz parmesan (grated).
- 1 tbsp butter.

Instructions

1. Heat the cream in a large saucepan; bring to a gentle boil and allow to reduce slightly.
2. Heat the butter in a large frying pan and cook the bacon until crispy; set aside and leave grease warming in the pan (low heat).
3. Add the mayonnaise to the cream and turn down the heat.
4. Using a potato peeler, make thin zucchini strips. Cook the zucchini noodles for 30 seconds in a pan of boiling water.
5. Add cream mixture and bacon fat to the zucchini noodles, tossing to ensure all are coated. Mix in the bacon and parmesan

Tuna & Cheese Oven Bake

TIME TO PREPARE

10 minutes

COOK TIME

25 minutes

SERVING

2 People

Nutrition per serving: Calories: 957, Protein: 44 g, Fat: 85 g, Net Carbs: 5 g

Ingredients	Instructions

Ingredients

- 16 oz tuna (tinned in olive oil).
- 5 oz celery (finely chopped).
- 4 oz parmesan (grated).
- 1 cup (230g) mayonnaise.
- One green bell pepper (diced).
- One onion (diced).
- 2 oz butter.
- 1 tsp chilli flakes.

Instructions

1. Preheat the oven to 200 degrees.
2. In a large frying pan, fry the celery, pepper, and onion until soft.
3. mix tuna, mayonnaise, parmesan, and chilli flakes until well combined.
4. Stir in the cooked vegetables; pour the mixture into an ovenproof dish.
5. Bake for 20-25 minutes or until golden brown.

Baked salmon

TIME TO PREPARE

10 minutes

COOK TIME

15 minutes

SERVING

4 People

Nutrition per serving: Calories: 354, Protein: 35 g, Fat: 23 g, Net Carbs: 1 g

Ingredients	Instructions

Ingredients

- 4 skinless salmon fillets
- 1 tbsp olive oil or melted butter
- chopped herbs, lemon slices and steamed long-stem broccoli to serve (optional)

Instructions

1. Heat the oven to 180C/160C fan/gas 4. Brush each salmon fillet with the oil or butter and season well.
2. Put the salmon fillets in an ovenproof dish. Cover if you prefer your salmon to be tender, or leave uncovered if you want the flesh to roast slightly.
3. Roast for 10-15 mins (or about 4 mins per 1cm thickness) until just opaque and easily flaked with a fork. Serve with a sprinkling of chopped herbs, lemon slices and steamed long-stem broccoli, if you like.

Herb omelette with fried tomatoes

TIME TO PREPARE

05 minutes

SERVING

2 People

COOK TIME

05 minutes

Nutrition per serving: Calories: 205, Protein: 17 g, Fat: 13 g, Net Carbs: 3 g

Ingredients	Instructions

- 1 tsp rapeseed oil
- 3 tomatoes, halved
- 4 large eggs
- 1 tbsp chopped parsley
  1 tbsp chopped basil

1. Heat the oil in a small non-stick frying pan, then cook the tomatoes cut-side down until softening and colouring. Meanwhile, beat the eggs in a small bowl with the herbs and plenty of freshly ground black pepper.
2. Scoop the tomatoes from the pan and put them on two serving plates. Pour the egg mixture into the pan and stir gently with a wooden spoon so the egg on the base of the pan moves to enable the uncooked egg to flow into the space. Stop stirring when it's nearly cooked to allow it to set into an omelette. Cut into four and serve with the tomatoes.

Salmon & Spinach Casserole

TIME TO PREPARE

10 minutes

COOK TIME

40 minutes

SERVING

4 People

Nutrition per serving: Calories: 640, Protein: 37 g, Fat: 54 g, Net Carbs: 5

Ingredients	Instructions

Ingredients

- 10 oz tinned salmon.
- 9 oz spinach (frozen).
- 1 ½ cups (150g) parmesan (grated).
- One cup (240g) of thick cream.
- ½ cup (120g) of almond milk.
- ¼ cup (55g) butter.
- Four slices of mozzarella.
- One garlic clove (crushed).
- 1 tbsp parsley (dried).

Instructions

1. Preheat the oven to 180 degrees.
2. In a large saucepan, heat the butter with the garlic. When garlic is browned, add in almond milk and cream.
3. Heat 5-6 minutes and stir in parmesan, spinach, parsley, and salmon.
4. Constantly stir until the mixture is bubbling.
5. Pour into an ovenproof dish and top with mozzarella cheese.
6. Bake for 25-30 minutes until bubbling and golden.

Creamy chicken stew

TIME TO PREPARE

10 minutes

COOK TIME

55 minutes

SERVING

4 People

Nutrition per serving: Calories: 400, Protein: 26 g, Fat: 27 g, Net Carbs: 6 g

Ingredients	Instructions

Ingredients

- 3 leeks, halved and finely sliced
- 2 tbsp olive oil
- 1 tbsp butter
- 8 small chicken thighs
- 500ml chicken stock
- 1 tbsp Dijon mustard
- 75g crème fraîche
- 200g frozen peas
- 3 tbsp dried or fresh breadcrumbs
- small bunch of parsley, finely chopped

Instructions

1. Tip the leeks and oil into a flameproof casserole dish on low heat, add the butter and cook everything gently for 10 minutes or until the leeks are soft.
2. Put the chicken, skin-side down, in a large non-stick frying pan on medium heat, cook until the skin browns, then turn and brown the other side. You shouldn't need any oil, but add a little if the skin starts to stick. Add the chicken to the leeks, leaving behind any fat in the pan.
3. Add the stock to the dish and bring to a simmer, season well, cover and cook for 30 mins on low. Stir in the mustard, crème fraîche and peas and bring to a simmer. It would be best if you had quite a bit of sauce.
4. When you're ready to serve, put the grill on. Mix the breadcrumbs and parsley, sprinkle them over the chicken and grill until browned.

Mushroom brunch

TIME TO PREPARE

5 minutes

COOK TIME

15 minutes

SERVING

4 People

Nutrition per serving: Calories: 154, Protein: 13 g, Fat: 11 g, Net Carbs: 1 g

Ingredients	Instructions

Ingredients

- 250g mushrooms
- 1 garlic clove
- 1 tbsp olive oil
- 160g bag kale
- 4 eggs

Instructions

1. Slice the mushrooms and crush the garlic clove. Heat the olive oil in a large non-stick frying pan, then fry the garlic over low heat for 1 min. Add the mushrooms and cook until soft. Then, add the kale. If the kale won't all fit in the pan, add half and stir until wilted, then add the rest. Once all the kale is wilted, season.
2. Now crack in the eggs and keep them cooking gently for 2-3 mins. Then, cover the eggs with the lid for 2-3 minutes or until they are cooked to your liking. Serve with bread.

Salmon Buttered Cabbage

TIME TO PREPARE

10 minutes

COOK TIME

25 minutes

✕ **SERVING**

4 People

Nutrition per serving: Calories: 768, Protein: 33 g, Fat: 70 g, Net Carbs: 3 g

Ingredients

- 16 oz salmon fillets (frozen & defrosted).
- 16 oz white cabbage.
- 4 oz butter.
- 2 oz shredded coconut (unsweetened).
- 5 tbsp olive oil.
- 1 tsp turmeric.
- ½ tsp onion powder.

Instructions

1. Cut the salmon into bite-size pieces and drizzle over olive oil.
2. mix coconut, turmeric, and onion powder in a small bowl. Dip each salmon chunk into the coconut mix until the salmon is well coated.
3. In a frying pan, fry the salmon until golden brown; cover with foil and set aside.
4. Melt the butter in the frying pan and fry the cabbage until it browns lightly.
5. Place the cabbage on a plate and the salmon on top; drizzle with olive oil

Mexican Salmon Fillets

TIME TO PREPARE

10 minutes

COOK TIME

20 minutes

SERVING

4 People

Nutrition per serving: Calories: 451, Protein: 33 g, Fat: 34.9 g, Net Carbs: 8 g

Ingredients	Instructions

Ingredients

- Four salmon fillets (frozen & defrosted).
- Two avocados (chopped into small cubes).
- 4 tsp Cajun seasoning.
- One jalapeno (finely diced).
- One onion (finely diced).
- 1 tbsp olive oil.
- 1 tbsp lime juice (fresh).
- 1 tbsp fresh coriander (finely diced).

Instructions

1. Season both sides of the salmon with Cajun seasoning.
2. Heat the oil in a frying pan; fry the salmon until browned, flip it, and repeat for the other side until it easily flakes with a fork.
3. Mix the avocados, onion, jalapenos, lime, and coriander until well combined.
4. Serve salmon and avocado mix together on a plate.

Keto Dinner Recipes

Grilled Chicken Thighs Rosemary

TIME TO PREPARE

10 minutes

COOK TIME

40 minutes

SERVING

4 People

Nutrition per serving: Calories: 465, Protein: 30 g, Fat: 36.2 g, Net Carbs: 2 g

Ingredients	Instructions

Ingredients

- 1½ lbs. (700g) chicken thighs
- Three tablespoons balsamic vinegar
- Three tablespoons extra virgin olive oil
- Three tablespoons minced garlic
- 1-½ teaspoons thyme
- Two teaspoons of chopped rosemary

½ teaspoon pepper

Instructions

1. Combine balsamic vinegar with extra virgin olive oil and season with minced garlic, thyme, pepper, and chopped rosemary.
2. Rub the chicken thighs with the spice mixture, then let it rest for approximately 15 minutes.
3. preheat a grill over medium heat, then wait until it is ready.
4. Place the seasoned chicken thighs on the grill until all chicken sides are golden brown and cooked. Brush the chicken thighs with the marinade once every 5 minutes.
5. Transfer the chicken from the grill to a serving dish.
6. Serve and enjoy warm.

Green Vegetable Soup

TIME TO PREPARE

05 minutes

SERVING

4 People

COOK TIME

20 minutes

Nutrition per serving: Calories: 150, Protein: 10 g, Fat: 15 g, Net Carbs: 7 g

Ingredients	Instructions

Ingredients

- 1 bunch spring onions, chopped
- 1 large potato, peeled and chopped
- 1 garlic clove, crushed
- 1l vegetable stock
- 250g (8.4 oz.) frozen peas
- 100g (3.4 oz.) fresh spinach
- 300ml natural yogurt
- A few mint leaves, basil leaves, cress or a mixture to serve

Instructions

1. Put the spring onions, potato and garlic into
2. a large pan. Pour over the vegetable stock and bring to the boil.
3. Reduce the heat and simmer for 15 minutes with a lid on or until the potato is soft enough to mash with the back of a spoon.
4. Add the peas and bring back up to a simmer. Scoop out around 4 tbsp of the peas and set aside for the garnish.
5. Stir the spinach and yoghurt into the pan, then carefully pour the whole mixture into a blender or use a stick blender to blitz it until it's smooth. Season to taste with black pepper.
6. Ladle into bowls, add some reserved cooked peas and scatter over your favourite soft herbs or cress. Serve with crusty bread, if you like.

Marinated Chicken Lemon Jalapeno

TIME TO PREPARE

10 minutes

COOK TIME

140 minutes

SERVING

4 People

Nutrition per serving: Calories: 396, Protein: 21.3 g, Fat: 31.6 g, Net Carbs: 6 g

Ingredients	Instructions

Ingredients

- 1-½ lbs. (700g) chicken thighs
- Four tablespoons extra virgin olive oil
- 2 cups (300g) chopped onion
- Two tablespoons minced garlic
- Three tablespoons chopped jalapeno
- Three tablespoons of lemon juice
- Two teaspoons thyme
- 1-teaspoon cinnamon

Instructions

1. Combine extra virgin olive oil with lemon juice and season with onion, jalapeno, minced garlic, thyme, and cinnamon. Stir well.
2. Store in the fridge to keep it fresh.
3. After 2 hours, remove the marinated chicken from the fridge and thaw at room temperature.
4. preheat a grill over medium heat, then wait until it is ready.
5. Place the marinated chicken thighs on the grill until cooked through. Occasionally, brush the chicken thighs with the remaining marinade.
6. Remove the grilled chicken thighs from the grill and arrange on a serving dish.
7. Serve and enjoy.

Chicken Stew with Baby Spinach

TIME TO PREPARE

10 minutes

COOK TIME

40 minutes

SERVING

4 People

Nutrition per serving: Calories: 410, Protein: 12.3 g, Fat: 34 g, Net Carbs: 2 g

Ingredients	Instructions

Ingredients

- 1 lb. (500g) chopped boneless chicken thighs
- Three tablespoons olive oil
- Two tablespoons garlic
- ½ teaspoon oregano
- ½ teaspoon pepper
- ½ cup (75g) halved cherry tomatoes
- 1 cup (250g) water
- ½ cup (120ml) of coconut milk
- 1 cup (30g) chopped baby spinach

Instructions

1. Preheat a skillet over medium heat, then add virgin olive oil.
2. Once it is hot, stir in minced garlic, then sauté until lightly golden and aromatic.
3. add chopped boneless chicken thighs to the skillet and sauté until the chicken is no longer pink.
4. Season the chicken with oregano and pepper, then pour water over the chicken. Bring to a boil.
5. Once it is boiled, reduce the heat and cook until the chicken is tender and the water is completely absorbed into the chicken.
6. Pour coconut milk into the skillet and add halved cherry tomatoes to the stew. Bring to a simmer.
7. add chopped baby spinach to the skillet and stir well once done.
8. Remove the chicken stew from the heat and transfer it to a serving dish.
9. Serve and enjoy warm.

Broccoli Cheddar Soup

TIME TO PREPARE

10 minutes

COOK TIME

20 minutes

SERVING

4 People

Nutrition per serving: Calories: 282, Protein: 12 g, Fat: 24 g, Net Carbs: 1 g

Ingredients	Instructions

Ingredients

- 2 tablespoons Butter
- 1/ 8 Cup (20g) White Onion
- 1/2 teaspoon Garlic
- 2 Cups (200g) Chicken Broth
- Salt and Pepper
- 1 Cup (70g) Broccoli, chopped into bite-size pieces
- 1 Tablespoon Cream Cheese
- 1/4 Cup (58g) Heavy whipping/double cream
- 1 Cup (112g) Cheddar Cheese; shredded

Instructions

1. In a large pot, saute onion and garlic with butter over medium heat until onions are softened and translucent.
2. Add broth and broccoli to the pot. Cook broccoli until tender. Add salt, pepper and desired seasoning.
3. Place cream cheese in a small bowl and heat in the microwave for ~30 seconds until soft and easily stirred.
4. Stir heavy whipping cream and cream cheese into soup; bring to a boil.
5. Turn off the heat and quickly stir in cheddar cheese.
6. Stir in xanthan gum, if desired. Allow to thicken.

Crispy Chicken with Cheese Sauce

TIME TO PREPARE

10 minutes

COOK TIME

40 minutes

SERVING

4 People

Nutrition per serving: Calories: 439.8, Protein: 12.4 g, Fat: 42.7 g, Net Carbs: 5.1 g

Ingredients	Instructions

Ingredients

- 1 lb. boneless chicken thigh
- ½ teaspoon black pepper
- 1 cup (112g) almond flour
- One egg
- ½ cup (120g) extra virgin olive oil to fry
- 1 cup (120g) almond yoghurt
- 1 cup (120g) grated cheddar cheese
- Two teaspoons mustard

Instructions

1. Cut the boneless chicken thigh into slices, then set aside.
2. Crack the egg, then place it in a bowl.
3. Season the egg with black pepper, then stir until incorporated.
4. Dip the sliced chicken in the beaten egg, then roll in the almond flour. Make sure that the chicken is completely coated with almond flour.
5. Preheat a frying pan over medium heat, then pour olive oil into the pan.
6. Once the oil is hot, put the chicken in the frying pan and fry until both sides of the chicken are lightly golden brown and the chicken is thoroughly cooked.
7. Place the crispy chicken on a serving dish.
8. In the meantime, place almond yoghurt, grated cheddar cheese, and mustard in a saucepan, then bring to a simmer over deficient heat.
9. Stir the sauce until incorporated, then remove from heat.
10. Drizzle the cheese sauce over the chicken, then serve.

Chili Chicken Tender with Fresh Basils

TIME TO PREPARE

15 minutes

COOK TIME

30 minutes

SERVING

4 People

Nutrition per serving: Calories: 410.3, Protein: 25.6 g, Fat: 31.5 g, Net Carbs: 4 g

Ingredients

- 2 lbs. (1kg) boneless chicken thighs
- Two tablespoons minced garlic
- Two lemon kinds of grass 2 cups water
- ¼ cup (50g) diced red tomatoes
- Two tablespoons red chilli flakes
- Three tablespoons extra virgin olive oil
- ½ cup (30g) fresh basils

Instructions

1. Cut the boneless chicken thighs into medium cubes, then place them in a skillet.
2. Season the chicken with minced garlic and lemon grasses, then pour water over the chicken. Bring to a boil.
3. Once it is boiled, reduce the heat and cook until the water is completely absorbed into the chicken.
4. Remove the cooked chicken from heat, then set aside.
5. preheat a saucepan over medium heat, then pour olive oil.
6. Stir in the chicken and cook until lightly brown.
7. Add red tomatoes, chilli flakes, and fresh basils to the saucepan, then stir until wilted and the chicken is thoroughly seasoned.
8. Transfer the chicken to a serving dish, then serve.
9. Enjoy!

Chicken Avocado Creamy Salad

TIME TO PREPARE

12 minutes

COOK TIME

30 minutes

SERVING

4 People

Nutrition per serving: Calories: 448.2, Protein: 16.5 g, Fat: 40 g, Net Carbs: 2 g

Ingredients	Instructions
• 1 lb. (500g) boneless chicken thighs • ½ cup (120ml) almond milk • 1-teaspoon oregano • Two tablespoons lemon juice • Three tablespoons extra virgin olive oil • One ripe avocado • Two tablespoons chopped celeries • Two tablespoons cilantro • ¼ cup (40g) diced onion • ¼ teaspoon pepper	1. Add oregano to the almond milk, then stir well. 2. Cut the boneless chicken thighs into slices, then rub them with almond milk. Let it rest for approximately 10 minutes. 3. preheat an oven to 250°F and line a baking tray with aluminium foil. 4. Spread the seasoned chicken on the prepared baking tray and bake until the chicken is done. 5. While waiting for the chicken, cut the avocado into halves, then remove the seed. 6. Peel the avocado, then cut into cubes. 7. Place the avocado cubes in a salad bowl, then drizzle lemon juice and extra virgin olive oil over the avocado. 8. Add chopped celery, cilantro, onion, and pepper to the salad bowl, then toss to combine. 9. Once the chicken is done, remove it from the oven and transfer it to a serving dish. 10. Top the chicken with avocado salad, then serve.

Strawberries smoothie

TIME TO PREPARE
05 minutes

COOK TIME
00 minutes

SERVING
2 People

Nutrition per serving: Calories: 74, Protein: 3 g, Fat: 8 g, Net Carbs: 4 g

Ingredients	Instructions

- 8 oz strawberries (frozen & defrosted).
- 8 oz blueberries (frozen & defrosted).
- One cup (227g) of Greek yoghurt (full fat).
- ½ cup thick or single whipping cream.
- 1 tsp orange extract.

1. Place all ingredients into a blender and mix until thoroughly combined.
2. Pour into a bowl and freeze for 40-60 minutes

Keto Chilli-Con-Carne

TIME TO PREPARE

15 minutes

COOK TIME

40 minutes

SERVING

4 People

Nutrition per serving: Calories: 529, Protein: 31.2 g, Fat: 40.2 g, Net Carbs: 7 g

Ingredients	Instructions

Ingredients

- 16 oz minced beef (frozen & defrosted).
- 1 ½ cups (250g) canned chopped tomatoes.
- 3 oz cheddar cheese (grated).
- Two garlic cloves (crushed).
- One red onion (diced).
- ½ red pepper (diced).
- ½ yellow pepper (diced).
- 2 tsp tomato puree.
- 2 tsp coriander.
- 1 tsp chilli powder.

Instructions

1. Preheat the oven to 180 degrees.
2. In a large frying pan, fry the onions and garlic cloves until tender. Stir in the beef and fry until browned and cooked through.
3. Add chopped tomatoes, red and yellow peppers, tomato puree, coriander, and chilli powder; fry for 6-7 minutes until bubbling.
4. Pour into an ovenproof dish and sprinkle cheese on top.
5. Bake for 25-30 minutes.

Almighty Almond Cheesecake

TIME TO PREPARE

10 minutes

SERVING

10 cakes

COOK TIME

50 minutes

Nutrition per serving: Calories: 529, Protein: 31.2 g, Fat: 40.2 g, Net Carbs: 7 g

Ingredients

- 24 oz cream cheese.
- Four large eggs.
- 1 cup (150g) stevia.
- ⅓ cup (80g) sour cream.
- ½ tsp almond extract.

Instructions

1. Preheat the oven to 175 degrees.
2. In a bowl, whisk the cream cheese until smooth, then gently add stevia, sour cream, and almond extract and mix until well combined.
3. Add the eggs individually and whisk until a thick, creamy mixture is formed.
4. Grease a springform pan, pour in the mixture, and bake for 45-50 minutes until puffed and lightly browned.
5. Remove from the oven and allow to sit at room temperature for an hour.
6. Place in the refrigerator for 5-6 hours.

Keto Blueberry Kefir Smoothie

TIME TO PREPARE

05 minutes

COOK TIME

5 minutes

SERVING

2 People

Nutrition per serving: Calories: 477, Protein: 4 g, Fat: 50 g, Net Carbs: 6 g

Ingredients	Instructions

Ingredients

- 1 1/2 cup (360ml) coconut milk kefir
- 1/2 cup (75g) blueberries, fresh or frozen
- 2 tbsp MCT oil or Brain Octane Oil
- 1/2 tsp pure vanilla powder or 1-2 tsp sugar-free vanilla extract (you can make your own)
- 1/2 cup (120 ml) water + ice cubes

Instructions

1. Place all the ingredients into a blender: kefir, blueberries, vanilla, MCT oil and ice.
2. Pulse until smooth.
3. Enjoy!

Crispy Almond Chicken with Tomato

TIME TO PREPARE

10 minutes

COOK TIME

20 minutes

SERVING

4 People

Nutrition per serving: Calories: 477, Protein: 4 g, Fat: 50 g, Net Carbs: 6 g

Ingredients	Instructions

Ingredients

- ¾ lb. (375g) boneless chicken thighs
- One egg
- ¼ cup (30g) almond flour
- ½ cup (120ml) extra virgin olive oil to fry
- 1 cup (150g) chopped onion
- ½ cup (112g) tomato puree
- ¼ teaspoon pepper

Instructions

1. Cut the boneless chicken thighs into thin slices, then set aside.
2. Crack the egg, then place it in a bowl. Beat until incorporated.
3. Dip the sliced chicken in the beaten egg, then roll in the almond flour. Repeat with the remaining chicken and almond flour.
4. After that, preheat a pan over medium heat, then pour olive oil into it.
5. Once the oil is hot, put the coated chicken into the pan, then fry lightly golden brown until the chicken is cooked through.
6. Discard the excessive oil.
7. Arrange the fried chicken on a serving dish, then set it aside.
8. Take two tablespoons of oil, then pour into a saucepan.
9. Stir in chopped onion, then sauté until lightly golden brown and aromatic.
10. add tomato puree to the saucepan, then season with pepper. Stir well and bring to a simmer.
11. Once it is done, remove the sauce from the heat, then drizzle the tomato sauce over the chicken.

Zingy Lemon & Lime Pancakes

TIME TO PREPARE

10 minutes

COOK TIME

20 minutes

SERVING

10 cakes

Nutrition per serving: Calories: 273, Protein: 9. g, Fat: 28 g, Net Carbs: 4 g

Ingredients

- Four eggs.
- 2 cups (220g) almond flour.
- ¼ cup (60ml) of water.
- 8 tbsp butter (melted).
- 2 tbsp swerve.
- 1 tbsp coconut oil.
- 1 tsp baking powder.
- One lime zest

Instructions

1. Place all ingredients in a blender and blend until well combined.
2. Allow resting for 10-15 minutes.
3. Heat a little oil in a frying pan and pour in ⅓ cup of the butter mixture.
4. Cook for 2-3 minutes on each side until golden brown.
5. Repeat the process until all of the batters have gone.

Creamiest Chocolate Dessert

TIME TO PREPARE

05 minutes

COOK TIME

60 minutes

SERVING

2 People

Nutrition per serving: Calories: 673, Protein: 15 g, Fat: 82 g, Net Carbs: 8 g

Ingredients	Instructions

Ingredients

- Two avocados (ripe).
- ¾ cup (180g) of thick or single cream.
- ½ cup (80g) of chocolate chips (unsweetened).
- ¼ cup (30g) swerve.
- 3 tbsp cocoa powder (unsweetened).
- 1 tsp vanilla extract.

Instructions

1. Mix all ingredients in a blender until smooth.
2. Transfer mixture into two serving bowls/glasses and refrigerate for 45-60 minutes.

Keto-Buzz Blueberry Pancakes

TIME TO PREPARE

10 minutes

SERVING

2 People

COOK TIME

10 minutes

Nutrition per serving: Calories: 132, Protein: 7 g, Fat: 7 g, Net Carbs: 4 g

Ingredients

- Three large eggs.
- ½ cup (60g) almond flour.
- ¼ cup (60ml) of milk.
- ¼ cup (50g) of fresh blueberries.
- 2 tbsp coconut flour.
- 2 tbsp sweetener (granulated).
- 1 tsp cinnamon (ground).
- ½ tsp baking powder.

Instructions

1. Add all ingredients (except blueberries) to a blender and mix until a thick batter is formed.
2. Add the blended mixture to a bowl and stir in blueberries.
3. Grease a large non-stick frying pan and allow the pan to get hot over medium heat.
4. Pour ¼ cup of the mixture into the hot pan and allow to cook for 2 - 3 minutes or until the edges start to crisp and turn lightly browned. Flip and repeat.
5. Repeat the process using the remaining batter.

Tasty Salted Turnip Fries

TIME TO PREPARE
10 minutes

COOK TIME
40 minutes

SERVING
4 People

Nutrition per serving: Calories: 219, Protein: 2 g, Fat: 22.2 g, Net Carbs: 7 g

Ingredients

- 16 oz turnips.
- 6 tbsp olive oil.
- 2 tsp onion powder.
- ½ tsp paprika.
  1 tsp salt.

Instructions

1. Preheat oven to 400 degrees.
2. Wash and peel the turnips; cut into ½ inch strips.
3. In a large bowl, toss the turnips in 2 tbsp of olive oil, salt, onion powder, and paprika.
4. Add remaining oil to a baking tray and heat in the oven for 5 minutes.
5. Bake for 25-30 minutes or until the fries are golden brown and crispy.

Tantalising Chocolate Truffles

TIME TO PREPARE

10 minutes

SERVING

4 People

COOK TIME

40 minutes

Nutrition per serving: Calories: 219, Protein: 2 g, Fat: 22.2 g, Net Carbs: 7 g

Ingredients	Instructions

Ingredients

- One avocado (mashed).
- One cup (160g) of chocolate chips (unsweetened & melted).
- ¼ cup (25g) of cocoa powder.
- 1 tsp vanilla extract.

Instructions

1. Mix avocado, chocolate, and vanilla extract until well combined and smooth.
2. Place in the refrigerator for 20-25 minutes until slightly firm.
3. Using a teaspoon, scoop out one chocolate truffle. Roll it in the palm of your hand to mould it to a round shape.
4. Roll in cocoa powder and repeat until all the chocolate mixture has gone.

Roasted cauliflower steaks

TIME TO PREPARE

10 minutes

COOK TIME

15 minutes

SERVING

2 People

Nutrition per serving: Calories: 277, Protein: 9 g, Fat: 21 g, Net Carbs: 7 g

Ingredients	Instructions

- 1 cauliflower
- ½ tsp smoked paprika
- 2 tbsp olive oil
- 1 roasted red pepper
- 4 black olives, pitted
- small handful of parsley
- 1 tsp capers
- ½ tbsp red wine vinegar
- 2 tbsp toasted flaked almonds

1. Heat oven to 220C/200C fan/gas 7 and line a baking tray with parchment. Slice the cauliflower into two 1-inch steaks – use the middle part as it's more extensive, and save the rest for another time. Rub the paprika and ½ tbsp oil over the steaks and season. Put on the tray and roast for 15-20 mins until cooked.
2. Meanwhile, make the salsa. Chop the pepper, olives, parsley and capers into a bowl and mix with the remaining oil and vinegar. Season to taste. When the steaks are cooked, spoon over the salsa and top with flaked almonds to serve.

CONCLUSION

One of the primary keys to any successful diet or lifestyle change has always been the recipes that fit in with the principles of the diet. I am sure there are many ways to achieve ketosis and to attain that weight loss goal. However, you do not want to get there by having the same old dishes repeatedly.

Variety is the game's name here, which is crucial in ensuring the sustainability of the ketogenic diet. The flavorful and delicious recipes in this step-by-step keto cookbook will be helpful additions for any keto dieter at any stage of their ketogenic journey. I have yet to see anyone complain about having too many easy yet delicious recipes!

ONE LAST THING...

If you enjoyed this book or found it helpful, I'd be very grateful if you'd post a short review on Amazon. Your support makes a difference, and I read all the reviews personally to get your feedback and make this book even better.

Thanks, again for your support!

Printed in Great Britain
by Amazon